I0816593

SKYBOX PRESS

METLIFE
CHAMPIONS

Canon

12
CenturyLink
45 KENNY EASLEY 81-87
17 DAVE KRIEG 80-91

FOREWORD

MARSHAWN LYNCH

Man, I can still remember my first game as a Seahawk in Seattle; it was HELLA loud. I felt at home running out that tunnel and onto the field 'cause I already had family out there that I played with back in college at Cal—Justin Forsett, Mike Gibson, Brandon Mebane, and Cameron Morrah—so we were already tapped in.

I played for 12 years off and on a few times, and I can say without a doubt that no other fanbase is more passionate than the 12s. Their love and energy is a game changer, for real. After I scored on what we all call the Beast Quake run in the 2010 Wild Card Game, the noise and shakin' was crazy. We didn't know then but we all know now that we created a f'n earthquake in that thang, what fanbase can make that happen?

Winning Super Bowl XLVIII put us on the map. Being up and out of the way in the Pacific Northwest, I think we got overlooked and maybe a little disregarded but winning that championship was big—not only for the team, but for the city, and that whole part of the country, ya' feel me? It changed the mindset: Seattle wasn't just about software and computers no more—you needed to be ready for what was coming out of the Pacific Northwest. And it was the way we did it, we didn't just win, we was smackin' people. There was no doubt. It was no fluke. We went and took it. The team, the organization, the city had the same mindset and we were not going to be denied.

I don't remember a lot of things from that victory parade but I do know there were like a million people from all walks of life, and a team is made up of individuals, but everyone came together as one that day. And so many people were throwing Skittles at my float that I felt bad for the street cleaners cause I know for sho' that it was gonna take hella long to clean all them up. Oh and another thing I do remember is that it was the first time I ever tried Fireball. I don't know who handed me the bottle but it was up.

If y'all didn't know, my go to is Hennessy, and I'd been enjoying a few while sitting at the crib and watching the game in December 2019 when running backs C.J. Prosise and Chris Carson both went down for the season. And then my phone rang; it was Mo Kelly [then VP of Player Engagement], asking if I had any more left in the tank because the Hawks needed a running back, and they wanted me to suit up. I thought it was a joke, but it was serious, so I put on that old number Two Fo' and got to finish my career as a Seattle Seahawk.

As the Seahawks celebrate their 50th anniversary, my message is simple. I believe you can't ever find the perfect words, and that it is most meaningful to be straight and to the point, so to the team, the city of Seattle, the Pacific Northwest, and all the 12s, I just want to say: Thank you. I know I speak for my teammates when I say - we appreciate everything.

SEAHAWKS
24

INTRODUCTION
BY STEVE RAIBLE

If it's true that it doesn't count as work if you love your job, then I've never worked a day in my life.

And I know it is true that time flies when you are having fun, because I have the unique distinction of having been with the Seahawks for all 50 years, and it's been an absolute blast.

I joined the expansion Seattle Seahawks in 1976 as a second-round draft pick (59th overall) out of Georgia Tech. A number of teams contacted leading up to the draft, including the Cowboys, the Bengals, and my favorite team growing up, the Packers. When the Seahawks drafted me, I had to ask where Seattle was. I knew it was in the Northwest, but coming from the Southeast, Seattle might as well have been somewhere in South Alaska.

I joke that I found out by carrier pigeon and arrived by Conestoga wagon. In fact, I arrived from Atlanta on what had been the longest flight of my life. I arrived on a day with clear, blue skies. I remember flying in and seeing the Smith Tower, the First Bank Tower, the waterfront, and of course the Kingdome. My first meal was at Ivar's Fish House on North end of Lake Union. It was love after my first flight.

I played wide receiver and tight end in college, and I felt confident about making the team. Four games into that first preseason, the Seahawks traded for another receiver named Steve. He was a fourth-round pick by Houston who wasn't able to crack the Oilers lineup, but we heard that he was a great guy and we'd be lucky to have him.

That other Steve figured he had a place with the Seahawks after he watched me one day at our old facility in Kirkland. Jim Zorn was throwing me passes at the end of practice; he had me run a six-yard slant, but I stumbled off my route, and the ball hit me on the helmet. The new guy saw this and said, "Oh, I can play here, no problem." That was my introduction to Steve Largent, with whom I became roommates and as close as brothers.

For an expansion team, we had some respectable records in those early years. We were 9–7 in our third and fourth seasons, but we didn't make the playoffs through the first five years. In our second exhibition game in 1981, I got hit in the ribs and suffered a collapsed lung. It took me two months before I could play again, and then, in our final game, I was covering a kickoff and tore ligaments in my ankle. The writing was on the wall. It was time to begin a new chapter.

During my six years in the NFL, I may have subconsciously been preparing for a career in broadcasting

after football, because for a guy who caught a grand total of just three career touchdowns, I wound up being one of the go-to interviews for reporters. Need a quote? How thick is your notebook?

One weekend, Seahawks broadcaster Pete Gross called the house while I was out playing in a charity golf tournament. Pete spoke to my wife, Sharon, and mentioned that there were job openings at KIRO-TV. He suggested I think about it and, if I were interested, to let him know in the next few weeks. Sharon said I'd be there ready to work on Monday!

I started as a color analyst with KIRO radio and backup sports anchor for KIRO-TV, eventually becoming the main evening news anchor. The games gave me a chance to appreciate from a different perspective how loud and supportive the 12s are. I got to stay around the game without having to deal with hits and the bruises and the injuries. Twenty-two years as the analyst gave way to the play-by-play job in 2004.

Most of my calls just came to me in the moment. I don't remember how I came up with "Holy Catfish!" The first time I said it, I was working with Warren Moon, and he looked over at me and said, "What the heck did you just say?" I mean, I couldn't say Holy Crap, and Holy Smoke felt overused, so it just came out as catfish.

When we beat the Carolina Panthers for our first NFC Championship in 2005, I was so happy for the fans and for coach Mike Holmgren, with whom I'd become friends. After 30 years, we were finally going to the Super Bowl. It was a tough loss, in part because you never know if or when you will get back again—but eight years later, I finally got to say those magic words: "Twelves, they're bringing the trophy home. Your Seahawks, Super Bowl 48 champions!"

During the victory parade, I remember looking at all the people who came out to celebrate, fans from near and far, of all different ages and races; the Seahawks brought everyone together. What a beautiful thing!

Over the past 50 years, I have missed only four Seahawks games (in 1981, when I was in the hospital recovering from that collapsed lung). I have travelled all around, and no city, team, and fans have a bond like Seattle, the Seahawks, and the 12s.

I have seen it all, and the players, the people, the highs and lows, the fan favorites, and the unforgettable moments that have made the first five decades of Seahawks football so memorable are all here in this keepsake book. I hope the 12s will enjoy looking back on the rich history while also looking forward to the bright future.

I know I am, which is why I like to say, "Save my parking spot, guys. I'm ready for 50 more!"

LUMEN
FIELD
SEAHAWKS
LUMEN
DELTA
ticketmaster
T Mobile

PREFACE
JOHN SCHNEIDER

The motivation behind every member of the Seahawks organization is our pride in representing the city of Seattle, the greater Pacific Northwest, and most of all, our fans. What makes the Seattle Seahawks unique is you, the 12s.

The atmosphere you create inside Lumen Field on game day is unmatched. And no matter where we go, you represent. The 12s presence is undeniable, and our opponents feel it too. You have played such a big role in our success that in 1984, we became the first team to retire a jersey in honor of the fans. How cool is that?

Every morning, we walk into the building with a simple approach: What are we doing to improve? From the coaches and the players to the entire front office, this mindset helps us work toward being a consistent championship-caliber team both on and off the field.

I'll never forget the day we brought the Lombardi Trophy home to Seattle—the energy, the love, and the overwhelming support during the parade. That memory fuels us each day as we work toward bringing another championship to this incredible city and fanbase.

From Chuck Knox to Pete Carroll. From Kenny Easley to Kam Chancellor. From Efren Herrera's unforgettable fake field goal to the seismic rumble of the Beast Quake—these aren't just legends and iconic moments, they are ingrained in the legacy of our franchise.

We hope that as you flip through this book, you relive the incredible players and awesome memories that connect you to this team. The bond between the Seahawks and the 12s is special, and we're dedicated to honoring that connection, ensuring that the next 50 years are as thrilling, if not more so, than the first.

CHAPTER ONE

1976-1982

Riddell

Seahawks cofounders Lloyd W. Nordstrom (left) and Herman Sarkowsky (right) with NFL Commissioner Pete Rozelle.

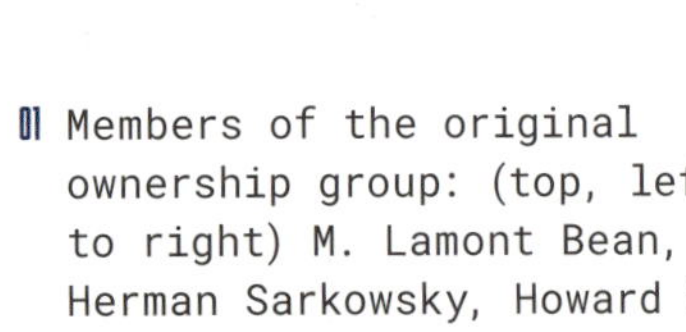

01 Members of the original ownership group: (top, left to right) M. Lamont Bean, Herman Sarkowsky, Howard S. Wright; (bottom, left to right) Elmer Nordstrom, Lynn P. Himmelman, D.E. "Ned" Skinner.

For those who have followed the Seahawks over the course of the franchise's history, it should come as no surprise that the special bond between the team and its passionate fan base actually predates the on-field product.

Before a Beast Quake led to measurable seismic activity during a playoff victory, before the NFL briefly tried out a rule preventing excessive crowd noise, in part due to the raucous crowds in the Kingdome, before 12s made so much noise at Super Bowl XLVIII that the game opened with a botched snap for a safety, setting the tone for a dominant victory, and before the No. 12 was retired in 1984 in honor of the fans, Seahawks fans were eager to support an expansion team that had not yet put on uniforms or played a snap.

After Seattle Professional Football Inc. was formed and secured the rights in 1974 to an expansion franchise to begin play in 1976, the fan frenzy quickly followed. More than 24,000 season-ticket applications were received on the first day, and in less than a month, the organization had sold nearly 60,000 season tickets to support a team that still hadn't been built. It was also the fans who selected the team's name, with "Seahawks" garnering the most votes out of the more than 20,000 fan submissions.

Of course, like fans of any expansion franchise, Seahawks fans would have to exercise patience at times, with the team going 2–14 in its inaugural season, then 5–9 in 1977. But under the no-nonsense leadership of head coach Jack Patera, a former NFL linebacker who oversaw the famous Purple People Eaters line as the defensive line coach of the Minnesota Vikings, the Seahawks improved quickly.

Following that pair of losing seasons, the Seahawks posted their first winning record, going 9–7 in 1978, with Patera winning Associated Press Coach of the Year honors.

01

SEATTLE HARDWARE COMPANY
ARMY MENS

02 The Kingdome was home to the Seahawks from 1976 to 1999.

That same year, general manager John Thompson's shrewd early acquisitions included trading an eighth-round pick to the Houston Oilers for receiver Steve Largent and signing a young, previously undrafted quarterback named Jim Zorn. With an exciting offense led by Zorn and Largent—the first two players named to the Seahawks Ring of Honor—the team repeated that 9–7 record in 1979 while thrilling fans with an attack that ranked fourth in points scored and seventh in total offense.

"It was fun," said tackle Nick Bebout, who played for the Seahawks from 1976 to 1979. "The first year, there were tense situations—it was a little hectic. Nobody really expected us to do much, and we didn't. It was a lot of hard work trying to build something from nothing. But we were the basis for what you have there today. I had some great times, some great memories in my four years in Seattle. It was super fun.

"We started to gain some respectability," he added. "People around the league started to take us a little more seriously. We laid some pretty good groundwork for the teams that followed, and the Seahawks have had some great years since then."

The Seahawks weren't able to immediately build on the success of their back-to-back nine-win seasons, posting losing records in each of the next three seasons before a coaching change was made in 1982, but despite some of those bumps in the road, the foundation for future success was being laid in the late 1970s and early 1980s.

In the 1980 draft, the Seahawks traded up in the first round to select Jacob Green with the 10th overall pick, and he would go on to become the team's all-time sack leader and a member of the Ring of Honor. The Seahawks also acquired a future Ring of Honor member in 1980 following the draft, signing quarterback Dave Krieg as an undrafted rookie out of Milton College, an NAIA school in Wisconsin that closed two years later.

The following year, the Seahawks used their first-round pick on UCLA safety Kenny Easley, who went on to earn AP NFL Defensive Player of the Year honors in 1984 and who eventually was enshrined in the Pro Football Hall of Fame. Easley, another Ring of Honor member, had his No. 45 retired by the team, one of only four players to receive that honor.

The Seahawks enjoyed only limited success in their early years under Patera and Thompson, but those seasons proved to be the building blocks for bigger things to come in the 1980s and beyond, and they laid the foundation for a relationship between fans and team that is one of the best in all of professional sports.

03

03 The first head coach of the Seahawks, Jack Patera, manned the sidelines for six-plus seasons.

04 Steve Niehaus wraps up Packers quarterback Lynn Dickey as Richard Harris closes in for the sack.

04

10
77

06

06 Steve Largent played his entire 14-year Hall of Fame career with the Seahawks.

07 Keith Butler was a mainstay at linebacker for Seattle from 1978 to 1987.

07

05 Jim Zorn fires a dart against the 49ers.

#80

STEVE LARGENT

WIDE RECEIVER

DATE INDUCTED
December 23, 1989

YEARS IN SEATTLE
1976–1989

COLLEGE
University of Tulsa

The inaugural inductee into the Ring of Honor in 1989, Steve Largent concluded his 14 National Football League seasons with league career records for receptions, 819; yards, 13,089; touchdowns, 100; consecutive games with a reception, 177; 50-catch seasons, 10; and 1,000-yard seasons, 8. Largent became the first Seahawks player to be elected to the Pro Football Hall of Fame, on July 29, 1995, and only the 23rd player to be elected in first year of eligibility. He finished in the AFC's (NFC in 1976) top 10 in receptions 10 times in his first 12 seasons. Led the AFC in receptions in 1978 with 71 and finished second in 1981 and 1987. Largent finished in the top 10 in receiving yards seven times, including a first-place finish in 1985, and second in 1978, missing the lead by one yard. Selected to play in the Pro Bowl seven times (1978, 1979, 1981, 1984, 1985, 1986, and 1987) and was first-team All-NFL (AP) in both 1979 and 1985. Largent led the team in both receptions and yards in each of the team's first 12 seasons. Third in games played (200) but has more starts (197) than any other player in Seahawks history. After retiring from the game in 1989, Largent would gain political aspirations and represented the 1st District of the State of Oklahoma for four terms. He would then serve and be re-elected for his home state in the United States House of Representatives before resigning in his first year of his fourth term to pursue the governorship of Oklahoma.

BJ

08 Safety Kenny Easley returns one of four Seahawks interceptions against the Raiders during a 34-21 Seahawks victory.

09 Defensive lineman Jacob Green stares down the Dolphins.

09

RING OF HONOR

#10

JIM ZORN

QUARTERBACK

DATE INDUCTED
August 3, 1991

YEARS IN SEATTLE
1976–1984

COLLEGE
Cal Poly Pomona

Inducted into the Ring of Honor in 1991, Jim Zorn was the starting quarterback for the Seahawks during their inaugural season in 1976 and would remain at the helm for the next seven years. Named the NFC Offensive Rookie of the Year in 1976 as he led the NFL in attempts with 439 and set a then-record 2,571 passing yards, which was also a record for an expansion team. By the end of the 1979 season, Zorn became only the third player to throw for 10,000 yards in his first four seasons. In 1978, he earned numerous accolades, which included being named AFC Player of the Year by the Washington D.C. Touchdown Club and first-team All-NFL by the NEA. Zorn is one of four Seahawks quarterbacks to throw for 300 yards in back-to-back games, which he accomplished twice, once in 1979 and again in 1981. Zorn finished his career leading the Seahawks in every passing category, amassing 20,122 passing yards and 107 touchdown passes.

10 Running back Sherman Smith ran for close to 3,500 yards in seven seasons with the Seahawks.

11 Efren Herrera's 46-yard field goal splits the uprights and gives Seattle a 17–16 victory over Oakland in 1978.

12 Defensive back John Harris lays out Oakland receiver Dokie Williams.

10

11

12

13 Defensive lineman Steve Niehaus was the first draft pick for the expansion Seahawks. Selected second overall, he earned NFC Defensive Rookie of the Year honors and set the Seahawks' rookie record for sacks in a season with 9.5 (before sacks became an official NFL statistic in 1982).

13

71
71

#22

DAVE BROWN

CORNERBACK

DATE INDUCTED
August 22, 1992

YEARS IN SEATTLE
1976–1986

COLLEGE
University of Michigan

Inducted into the Ring of Honor in 1992, Dave Brown was an 11-year starter in the Seahawks secondary from 1976 to 1986. Coming over from the Pittsburgh Steelers in the Veteran Allocation Draft in 1976, Brown played at the free safety position, leading the team with four interceptions. The following season, No. 22 would shift over to the right-side cornerback position, where he would be the "cornerstone" of the Seahawks defense for the next 10 years, picking off another 46 passes, retiring as the all-time Seahawks leader in the category with 50. In 1984, Brown picked off eight passes and was named to the AFC Pro Bowl squad and first-team All-NFL by NFL Films. Two of those interceptions were part of an NFL-record four interception returns for touchdowns on November 4, 1984, against the Kansas City Chiefs. Brown had returns of 90 and 58 yards. Brown retired as the Seahawks leader in interception return yards (643), interception returns for touchdowns (5), and the aforementioned interceptions (50).

22

CHAPTER TWO

1983-1991

The Seahawks headed into their second decade looking to make the leap from scrappy startup franchise to legit contender, but after a pair of winning seasons in 1978 and 1979, they took a step back, posting losing records in three straight seasons, ultimately leading to a coaching change during the 1982 campaign.

Looking to take the next step as a franchise, the Seahawks turned to one of the most successful coaches of the era, hiring Chuck Knox, a coach who had led both the Los Angeles Rams and the Buffalo Bills to division titles in the past decade.

And in a fitting turn, the team coached by a man nicknamed Ground Chuck traded up in the first round of the 1983 draft in order to select Penn State running back Curt Warner. The move would prove to be an inspired one, as Warner, an eventual Seahawks Ring of Honor selection, rushed for 1,449 yards and 13 touchdowns as a rookie, earning Pro Bowl and second-team All-Pro honors to help lead the Seahawks to a 9–7 record and the first playoff berth in franchise history.

That season also saw the Seahawks begin the transition from one Ring of Honor quarterback to another, with Dave Krieg, signed as an undrafted rookie out of Milton College in 1980, taking over the starting job from Jim Zorn midway through the season.

The Seahawks' 1983 season culminated in a trip to the AFC Championship Game, where Seattle beat the Denver Broncos at home in the Wild Card round before pulling off a big upset over the Dolphins in Miami, a win that remained the only road playoff win in franchise history until the 2012 team won a Wild Card game at Washington.

"We had started the franchise on pretty good footing, but then sort of stumbled there in the early '80s, and that's when Chuck came in," said receiver Steve Largent. "He righted the ship, so to speak. He had a plan and he executed it to perfection. We went to the playoffs the first year he was in Seattle, and that was the first time we made the playoffs, so that was really substantial. And he always had high goals. He set high standards for the team every year—if we were 8–8, that wasn't a good year at all. He always commanded the best from the players who played for him."

The 1984 season included a couple of significant milestones, most notably a then-franchise best 12–4

01 General manager Mike McCormack and head coach Chuck Knox prior to the 1983 NFL Draft. The Seahawks traded up to the third pick to select running back Curt Warner.

01 ◄

record. That was also the year the Seahawks retired No. 12, making them the first professional sports franchise to retire a number in honor of their fans.

The Seahawks missed the playoffs in 1985 and 1986, though they did go 10–6 in 1986. Knox then had his team back in the postseason in 1987 and 1988, and the 1988 squad claimed the first division title in team history.

1988 brought new ownership when Ken Behring and Ken Hofmann bought the team from the Nordstrom family, a move John Nordstrom would later say he came to regret after Behring attempted to relocate the team to Anaheim in 1996.

In addition to the winning records and playoff berths, the Knox era was also defined by the star power those teams had, led by Hall of Famers Steve Largent and Kenny Easley.

Largent, who the Seahawks got for the bargain price of an eighth-round pick in 1976, made the Pro Bowl seven times in his career, including four straight seasons from 1984 to 1987, and the 1985 season also saw him earn first-team All-Pro honors after leading the NFL with 1,287 receiving yards. By the time Largent retired in 1989, he was the league's all-time leader in receptions (819), receiving yards (13,089), and receiving touchdowns (100).

Easley, meanwhile, became one of the league's best and most feared defensive players in the 1980s, earning Pro Bowl honors five times and first-team All-Pro honors three times before his career was cut short due to kidney disease. In 1984, Easley was named Associated Press Defensive Player of the Year, making him the

03

02 Undrafted out of Milton College in his home state of Wisconsin, quarterback Dave Krieg signed with Seattle in 1980 and went on to enjoy a productive NFL career, playing 19 seasons—12 with the Seahawks.

03 The Seahawks became the first professional sports franchise to retire a jersey number in honor of their fans when, in 1984, the team officially retired number 12.

first Seahawks player, and to this day one of only two Seahawks, to earn that honor.

In addition to Largent, Easley, Warner, Zorn, and Krieg, the 1980s teams featured the likes of Ring of Honor defensive end Jacob Green, the team's all-time sack leader, and Ring of Honor cornerback Dave Brown, who was with the franchise from its inaugural season through 1986, earning Pro Bowl honors in 1984 and second-team All-Pro recognition in 1984 and 1985.

Another big name from that era, though one who did not ultimately reach his expected heights, was linebacker Brian Bosworth, aka the Boz, who the Seahawks selected in the 1987 Supplemental Draft after winning a lottery to get the top pick. Although Bosworth's career was cut short after just 24 games, he was a memorable character from that era.

The end of the 1980s brought another big change to the organization, as former Raiders coach Tom Flores took over as the team's president and general manager in 1989, a move that would be followed two years later by Flores replacing Knox as head coach following the 1991 season.

04 A first-round pick in the 1982 NFL Draft, defensive lineman Jeff Bryant played his entire 12-year career with Seattle.

05 Fullback Dan Doornink scoops up a blocked field goal attempt.

06 Head coach Chuck Knox celebrates on the shoulders of his players after a divisional-round win over Miami in 1983.

04

05

06

07 In that playoff win over Miami, Curt Warner led the Seahawks with 113 rushing yards and two touchdowns.

07 →

BIKE
28

#28

CURT WARNER

RUNNING BACK

DATE INDUCTED
November 27, 1994

YEARS IN SEATTLE
1983–1989

COLLEGE
Penn State University

Curt Warner was inducted into the Ring of Honor on November 27, 1994, after a career that spanned seven years from 1983 to 1989 and saw him hold every Seahawks rushing record when he was done. Immediately thrust into the Seahawks lineup his rookie season, Warner would rush for 1,449 yards and 13 touchdowns, highlighted by a then-Seahawks-record 207-yard effort against Kansas City. The season was capped off by being named a starter in the Pro Bowl, 1983 AFC Player of the Year by the Washington D.C. Touchdown Club and NFLPA, AFC Offensive Player of the Year by the NFLPA and UPI, second-team All-NFL by the AP and *Football Digest*, and first-team All-Rookie by *Pro Football Digest* and *Pro Football Weekly.* After suffering a season-ending injury in the first game of 1984, Curt would bounce back in 1985, rushing for 1,094 yards and being named the NFL's Comeback Player of the Year by *Sports Illustrated*. Warner would not look back his final three seasons, leading the team in rushing each year, averaging 1,164 yards a season and 10 touchdowns, including a then-Seahawks-record four touchdowns vs. Denver in 1988. Warner would be named to two more Pro Bowls (1986–87), bringing his career total to three, and was named AFC Offensive Player of the Year by the UPI in 1986 and first-team All-NFL by *Sports Illustrated* in 1987. He finished his career with 6,705 yards rushing on 1,649 carries with 62 touchdowns. He is currently second all-time in Seahawks history in attempts (1,649), third in rushing yards (6,705) and touchdowns (55), and fourth in total touchdowns (62).

55

08 The Boz. Colorful character and fan favorite Brian Bosworth was selected first overall by Seattle in the 1987 NFL supplemental draft, but a shoulder injury cut his career short after two full seasons and just 24 games.

09

10

11

09 Steve Largent beats Chargers DB Daniel Hunter for a touchdown.

10 Norm Johnson holds the Seahawks records for most points scored (810) and most games played by a kicker (134).

11 Cornerback Terry Taylor bats down a pass intended for Broncos receiver Sam Graddy.

#79

JACOB GREEN

DEFENSIVE END

DATE INDUCTED
September 3, 1995

YEARS IN SEATTLE
1980–1991

COLLEGE
Texas A&M University

Jacob Green became the second Seahawks defensive player to be inducted into the Ring of Honor on September 3, 1995. Green was a fixture at the left defensive end position for 12 years (1980–91). From the time the NFL made it an official statistic in 1982 until his retirement, Jacob was the third-most-productive sack artist in the game, trailing only the likes of Lawrence Taylor and Reggie White. In 1983, Green registered a single-game Seahawks-record 3.5 sacks against the Los Angeles Raiders and the NFL's longest interception return for the season, a 73-yard touchdown at Cleveland. The following year, Green equaled a team-record four fumble recoveries and registered a then-playoff-record 2.5 sacks in a Wild Card game against the Los Angeles Raiders. Green's career was highlighted by two Pro Bowl selections in 1986 and 1987. In 1986, he set a Seattle record with 4.0 sacks vs. the Giants. Green can be found scattered all over the Seahawks record book, having played in the fifth-most games (178) and had the third-most starts (176), most fumble recoveries (17), seventh-most tackles (718), and most career sacks (116.0).

12
79
50

12 Joe Terry and Jacob Green smother Raiders quarterback Rusty Hilger.

13 Melvin Jenkins intercepts a pass in the 1987 Wild Card game against the Houston Oilers.

13

RING OF HONOR

#45

KENNY EASLEY

SAFETY

DATE INDUCTED
October 14, 2002

YEARS IN SEATTLE
1981–1987

COLLEGE
UCLA

Kenny Easley was inducted into the Ring of Honor on October 14, 2002, with a sellout crowd and millions watching the *Monday Night Football* halftime ceremony at home, and elected to the Pro Football Hall of Fame on February 4, 2017. Easley redefined the strong safety position in seven years from 1981 from 1987. Voted by the Associated Press as the NFL Defensive Player of the Year in 1984, Easley had 32 interceptions in his storied career. This fierce hitter registered 107 tackles and three interceptions and returned an interception 82 yards vs. Cleveland in his rookie campaign, earning him AFC Rookie of the Year by the NFL Players' Association. The following season, Easley would earn the first of five Pro Bowl appearances, including being named a starter from 1983 to 1985 and again in 1987. The crowning jewel of Easley's career came in 1984, where he spearheaded the NFL's sixth-rated defense, which culminated into a Seahawks-record 12 wins in the regular season and a Wild Card victory over the rival Los Angeles Raiders. He tied a Seahawks team record by intercepting 10 passes, including three against San Diego on October 29. Easley would be named first-team All-NFL by the Associated Press for the second year in a row and was bestowed that honor again in 1985. Easley finished his career with 498 tackles, eight sacks, 10 forced fumbles, 11 fumble recoveries, and 32 interceptions.

14 Steve Largent receives a hug from his mother, Sue, during a ceremony honoring the Seahawks great prior to the final game of his Hall of Fame career.

15 Linebacker Fredd Young earned Pro Bowl honors in each of his four seasons in Seattle.

16 Edwin Bailey anchored the left guard position for the Seahawks through the 1980s.

15

14

16

17 Paul Skansi achieved folk hero status in 1990 when he caught a 25-yard desperation pass from Dave Krieg for a game-winning touchdown in the final seconds against the Chiefs.

#17

DAVE KRIEG

QUARTERBACK

DATE INDUCTED
September 26, 2004

YEARS IN SEATTLE
1980–1991

COLLEGE
Milton College

Dave Krieg became the eighth member of the Seahawks Ring of Honor on September 26, 2004. Krieg spent the first 12 years (1980–91) of his 19-year NFL playing career with the Seahawks while becoming the club's all-time leader in 31 career, season, and single-game passing categories at the time of his departure. Krieg originally joined the Seahawks as an undrafted free agent from Milton College in 1980 and became the regular starter nine games into the 1983 season. The three-time Pro Bowler (1984, 1988, and 1989) was the only Seattle quarterback with a playoff victory and led the Seahawks to their only conference championship game in 1983, a club-record 12 wins and the playoffs in 1984, and back-to-back playoff appearances again in 1987 and 1988, since matched and surpassed by Matt Hasselbeck and Russell Wilson.

BUSH
17
17

32
BRYAN
77

19

19 After starting his career lined up at tackle, Bryan Millard flourished playing guard during his eight-year NFL career, all as a Seahawk.

20 Another career Seahawk, Jeff Bryant was an iron man on the defensive line, starting 167 of the 175 games he played.

20

18 Fullback John L. Williams evades an Atlanta tackler deep in Seahawks territory.

CHUCK KNOX

HEAD COACH

DATE INDUCTED
September 25, 2005

YEARS IN SEATTLE
1983–1991

LEGACY
Four-Time NFL Coach of the Year

Chuck Knox was the ninth member inducted to the Ring. He spent nine of his 22 illustrious seasons at the helm of the Seahawks from 1983 to 1991, during which time he led Seattle to 80 wins en route to becoming the winningest coach in club history, since surpassed by Mike Holmgren and Pete Carroll. Compared to 63 losses, his winning percentage of .559 stood as the best for nearly three decades, with at least eight seasons coached. Knox posted six winning seasons with Seattle and led the Seahawks into postseason play four times. The Seahawks' three playoff wins under Knox were the only postseason wins in club history until 2005. Knox was named NFL Coach of the Year following both the 1983 and 1984 seasons, where Seattle posted a 21–11 record, advanced to the 1983 AFC Championship Game, and in 1984 posted the best record in franchise history at the time with a 12–4 mark. One of the NFL's all-time winningest coaches, Knox ranks 10th in league history with 193 career victories (193–158), including playoffs. He was the first coach in NFL history to lead three different franchises to the playoffs and was named NFL Coach of the Year four times while coaching three different teams (L.A. Rams, 1973; Bills, 1980; Seahawks, 1983–84).

Seattle
Seahawks

CHAPTER THREE

1992-1998

Riddell
SEATTLE
2 5
SEAHAWKS
adidas

The 1990s were a massive decade for Seattle, as the Emerald City found itself at the forefront of popular culture and technology.

Pearl Jam, Nirvana, Soundgarden, Alice in Chains, and other Seattle bands turned grunge into a global phenomenon and made the Pacific Northwest the center of the music universe. Seattle was also depicted in film and on television, from *Singles* and *Sleepless in Seattle* in movie theaters to *Frasier* and *The Real World* on the small screen. And a city long known best in the business world as the home of Boeing saw Starbucks and Microsoft grow into global brands in the 1990s, while a small tech company called Amazon also got its start there.

The 1990s were not, however, peak years for the Seahawks, as the team struggled through much of the decade. But just as future global brands got their start during those years, the groundwork for significant success was laid that decade for pro football in Seattle, even if the payoff didn't come until the 2000s.

After moving on from Chuck Knox in 1991, the Seahawks went just 2–14 in 1992 under Tom Flores, though that team did feature a great defense led by future Hall of Fame defensive tackle Cortez Kennedy, who won Associated Press Defensive Player of the Year honors despite the team's poor record, thanks to a dominant season that saw him record 14 sacks, 92 tackles, four forced fumbles, and a fumble return touchdown.

The Seahawks went 6–10 in each of their next two seasons before another coaching change brought Dennis Erickson back to the Pacific Northwest. Erickson, an Everett, Washington, native who had coached at Idaho and Washington State, was coming off a successful run at the University of Miami before the Seahawks brought him to the NFL. Erickson's teams were competitive but couldn't quite get over the hump, going 8–8 in three of his four seasons and 7–9 in the other.

The 1990s also saw the Seahawks acquire some bigtime talent led by Kennedy, who was acquired with the No. 3 pick in the 1990 draft after the Seahawks traded up. The decade also included top picks like Joey Galloway, the eighth overall pick in 1995, and both Shawn Springs and future Hall of Fame tackle Walter Jones in 1997, as well as free agent signings such as Ricky Watters, Chad Brown, and former Husky and eventual Hall of Famer Warren Moon.

01 Tom Flores joined the Seahawks as president and general manager in 1989. In 1992, he moved to the sidelines as head coach while retaining his duties as GM.

01 →

Riddell
84
Riddell
84

02 A first-round draft pick of the Seahawks, receiver Joey Galloway averaged better than 1,000 yards over his first four seasons in the NFL.

But no player addition in the 1990s was as big as the transaction that took place in 1997 when Paul Allen bought the team from Behring. The previous year, Behring had announced his plans to move the team to Anaheim, Califronia, causing local leadership to look for a new owner. Allen, the Microsoft cofounder who already owned the Portland Trail Blazers, wasn't initially interested in owning an NFL team as well, but ultimately, he decided to step up for his hometown and save the team from relocation.

"At the end of the day, there was no Plan B," King County Councilmember Pete von Reichbauer said in 2017, 20 years after Allen purchased the team. "There was only Plan A, and Plan A was Paul Allen. Nobody in this community wanted to buy the franchise.

"In the end, it wasn't a financial decision." he added. "It was a decision of commitment, and I go back to the fact that this is an Allen family commitment to this community, because there was no financial reason for him to buy the team, and there was no personal reason for him to buy the team. Paul Allen, he was not the last person standing—he was the only person standing. And he made a commitment not based upon a financial reward, not based upon anything personal; he based it on the values that his mom and dad taught him, and we owe as much to Faye and Ken Allen as we do Paul."

And once Allen decided to buy the team, his commitment to winning was obvious. Before he even completed the purchase of the team, a transaction that depended on the passing of Referendum 48 in 1997 to fund a new stadium, he signed off on the cost of paying for a pair of top 10 picks, paving the way for the Seahawks to make the trades they used to select Springs third overall and Jones sixth overall.

Allen made another big move following the 1999 season, hiring Mike Holmgren, who had previously led the Packers to two Super Bowls (winning one), as Seattle's new head coach, setting the Seahawks up for previously unseen levels of success the following decade.

The 1990s also marked the end for an iconic structure in Seattle, the Kingdome, which had been home to the Seahawks and the Mariners for more than two decades, as well as the host venue for three Final Fours, the Pro Bowl, Major League Baseball's All-Star Game, and the National Basketball Association's All-Star Game. The 1999 season was Seattle's last in the Kingdome before it was imploded in March 2000, making room for what is now Lumen Field.

That decade also saw the Seahawks say goodbye to Pete Gross, the voice of the Seahawks from 1976 to 1992. Gross died of cancer in 1992 just days after being inducted into the team's Ring of Honor.

03 Rick Tuten is one of two Seahawks punters selected to the Pro Bowl. He also received the honor of being named Seahawks Man of the Year for his leadership and community involvement.

04 Everett native Dennis Erickson returned home to coach the Seahawks for four seasons in the late 1990s.

05 Brian Blades scored eight touchdowns as a rookie and went on to be a go-to receiver for more than a decade in Seattle.

03

04

05

06 During a dominant three-year stretch from 1993 to 1995, running back Chris Warren averaged more than 1,300 rushing yards and was named to the Pro Bowl all three seasons.

06

#96

CORTEZ KENNEDY

DEFENSIVE TACKLE

DATE INDUCTED
September 17, 2006

YEARS IN SEATTLE
1990–2000

COLLEGE
University of Miami

Cortez Kennedy became the 10th member inducted into the Seahawks Ring of Honor on September 17, 2006, and was elected to the Pro Football Hall of Fame on February 4, 2012. Kennedy established himself as one of the premier interior defensive linemen in the game while playing 11 NFL seasons (1990–2000), all with the Seahawks. He appeared in eight Pro Bowls and a franchise-record six consecutive Pro Bowls (1991–96), including four as a starter. The three-time All-Pro is found throughout the Seahawks record books, finishing his career ranking sixth on the club's all-time list in games played (167), sixth in games started (153), and eighth in tackles (668). Kennedy ranks fourth in sacks (58), yards lost on sacks (392.0), and forced fumbles (13). His finest season came in 1992, when he became the second Seahawks player to win the Associated Press NFL Defensive Player of the Year Award (Kenny Easley, 1984) after recording 93 tackles (76 solo), 14.0 sacks, five forced fumbles, and four fumble recoveries. The 1999 co–defensive captain, Kennedy helped lead Seattle back to the postseason for the first time since 1988.

Riddell

07 Free safety Eugene Robinson struck an imposing presence in the Seattle defensive backfield for 11 seasons.

08

09

10

08 Strong safety Robert Blackmon tallied 15 interceptions in his seven seasons with the Seahawks.

09 Shawn Springs was selected third overall in the 1997 NFL Draft, the highest ever for a defensive back by Seattle.

10 Highly touted quarterback Rick Mirer set rookie franchise records for most passing attempts, completions, and yards (later topped by Russell Wilson), and he was only the third rookie QB in a quarter-century to start all 16 games.

PETE GROSS

PLAY-BY-PLAY RADIO ANNOUNCER

DATE INDUCTED
November 30, 1992

YEARS IN SEATTLE
1976–1992

LEGACY
Pete Gross House

Inducted into the Seahawks Ring of Honor in 1992, Pete Gross served as the radio play-by-play for 17 seasons, from the Seahawks' inaugural 1976 season through 1992. He is one of the most-beloved people to have ever been associated with the Seahawks franchise, and fans will never forget his numerous "touchdown Seahawks" calls. Over his 17 seasons, Gross called all but the five games he missed in 1992 while battling cancer. His career included eight playoff games, and in the 1983 season, Gross came within one game of the Super Bowl when Seattle faced the Los Angeles Raiders in the AFC Championship Game. The Seahawks lost that game, 30–14. Gross was diagnosed with cancer in 1989. He succumbed to the disease in 1992, just two days after his induction into the Ring. He was inducted into the Ring during a Monday night game versus the Denver Broncos, a game the 2–14 Seahawks won in overtime. Prior to moving to the Seahawks, he was the play-by-play voice of the University of Washington in both football and basketball. He came to Seattle after calling play-by-play for the University of the Pacific. Gross' legacy remains; the Seahawks are actively involved with the Pete Gross House. The Pete Gross House, which opened in November of 1999, is a 69-unit apartment complex that provides housing for families with members undergoing treatment at the Fred Hutchinson Cancer Research Center. The Pete Gross House is also the location of the Hutch School, a fully accredited K-through-12 school for cancer patients and their siblings. The Seahawks took an active role in seeing the project through to completion and participate in an annual fundraiser for the continued upkeep of the facility.

11 Defensive tackle Joe Nash holds the franchise record for most games played, having taken the field 218 times from 1982 to 1996.

12 Linebacker Rufus Porter struck fear in opposing offenses for seven seasons in Seattle.

12

13 University of Washington star quarterback Warren Moon played two seasons in Seattle toward the end of his Hall of Fame career, earning Pro Bowl honors at age 41.

14 Defensive end Michael Sinclair led the league in sacks (16.5) and forced fumbles (6) in 1998. His 16.5 sacks remain the single-season franchise record.

15 Kicker Todd Peterson hit 81.8% of his field goals and 100% of his extra points in five years with the Seahawks.

13

14

15

16 Running back Ricky Watters averaged more than 1,200 yards in three full seasons in Seattle.

16

Riddell
32

KINGDOME

STADIUMS

KINGDOME
1976–1999

HUSKY STADIUM
1994, 2000–2001

LUMEN FIELD
2002–Present

HUSKY STADIUM

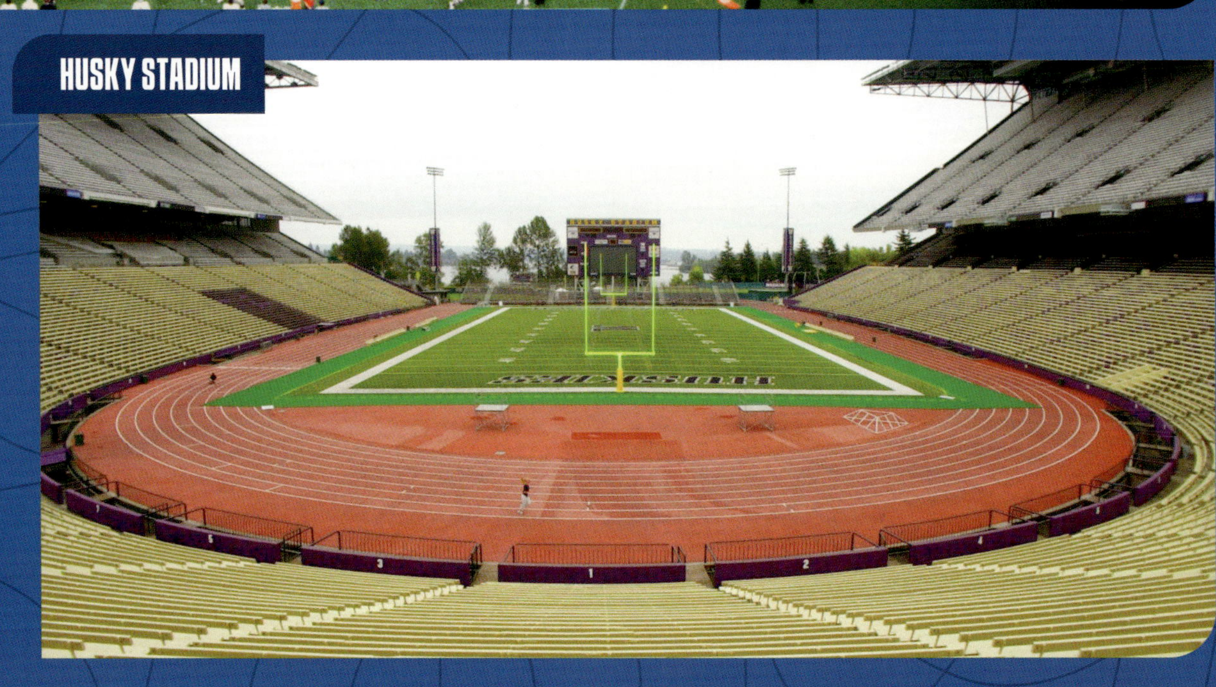

LUMEN FIELD

CHAPTER FOUR

1999–2009

Riddell
SEAHAWKS
37
XL
Riddel
SEAHAWKS
71

When Mike Holmgren was hired as the Seahawks' new head coach after the 1998 season, he was joining a franchise that had just finished its 10th straight season without a playoff appearance. Holmgren, however, was up to the task of turning around a struggling franchise, having done the same thing in Green Bay in the 1990s. There, he had taken over a team that had been to the playoffs just twice in its previous 24 seasons before his arrival and led them to six consecutive playoff berths from 1993 to 1998, including two Super Bowl appearances, one of which resulted in victory.

Holmgren helmed the Seahawks to a division title in his first season in Seattle, ending a decade-long playoff drought. With Tacoma native Jon Kitna at quarterback, the Seahawks went 9–7 during that 1999 season, the team's last at the Kingdome, before losing to Miami in the playoffs in what would be the final Seahawks game played in the team's original home.

The following offseason saw the Seahawks add, in the first round of the draft, running back Shaun Alexander, who would go on to become the franchise's all-time leading rusher and the only player in team history to win the NFL's MVP honors.

The Seahawks spent the 2000 and 2001 seasons playing home games at Husky Stadium as what is now known as Lumen Field was being constructed on the site of the Kingdome. The Seahawks missed the playoffs each of those years but saw some young stars begin to emerge, including Alexander, who rushed for 1,318 yards and an NFL-leading 14 touchdowns in 2001, and left tackle Walter Jones, who was named first-team All-Pro for the first time that season—an honor he would receive three more times, along with nine Pro Bowl selections, on his way to the Hall of Fame.

The 2001 season was also Matt Hasselbeck's first in Seattle after Holmgren, who had coached Hasselbeck as a backup in Green Bay, made a trade to bring him to Seattle. It took Hasselbeck a couple of seasons to really hit his stride, but he eventually developed into a three-time Pro Bowler who led the Seahawks to their first Super Bowl and was eventually named to the Seahawks Ring of Honor.

The following year brought a lot of change for the Seahawks, who in 2002 moved into their new home, Seahawks Stadium (now Lumen Field), moved from the AFC West to the NFC West, and debuted a new logo

01 Mike Holmgren acknowledges the 12s following his final home game as head coach in 2008.

01

NFC-WEST

and color scheme. That season, Seattle fell short of the postseason for the third straight year, but the pieces were being put into place for Holmgren's Seahawks to become one of the best teams in the NFC.

In 2003, they went 10–6 and returned to the playoffs. That season, the Seahawks unveiled a flagpole in the south end of the stadium, beginning the unique pregame tradition of having someone raise the 12 Flag just before kickoff.

In 2004, Seattle won its first NFC West title, the first of four consecutive division wins, as the Seahawks made the postseason for five straight seasons from 2003 to 2007, matching the total number of playoff berths in the franchise's history up to that point.

The 2005 season represented the peak of the Holmgren era, as the team finished 13–3, the best record in franchise history up to that point, earning the NFC's top seed. With homefield advantage on their side, the Seahawks beat the Washington Redskins in the divisional round, the team's first playoff win since the 1984 season, then beat the Carolina Panthers in the NFC Championship Game to secure the first Super Bowl berth in franchise history.

That season featured standout play from Hasselbeck and an MVP season for Alexander, who led the NFL with 1,880 rushing yards while scoring a then–NFL record 28 total touchdowns, as well as dominant play from the best offensive line in team history, a group that included two Hall of Famers in Jones and left guard Steve Hutchinson. Joining those four in earning Pro Bowl honors that season were rookie linebacker Lofa Tatupu,

03

center Robbie Tobeck, and fullback Mack Strong, giving the Seahawks seven Pro Bowl selections, matching the franchise-best total set by the 1984 team.

In 2007, the Seahawks won their fourth-straight division title as Hasselbeck threw for a then–franchise record 3,966 yards, and in that 10–6 season, Holmgren became the team's all-time winningest coach, a record later eclipsed by Pete Carroll.

The later years of the decade were a time of significant transition for the Seahawks. Alexander, who later was named to the Seahawks Ring of Honor, played his final game in 2007, while Walter Jones ended his Hall of Fame career in 2008, playing his final game on Thanksgiving before a knee injury ended his season. He would try to return for the 2009 season but was placed on injured reserve and announce his retirement in spring 2010.

Holmgren then stepped down as head coach after the 2008 season, handing the reins to Jim Mora, who had been named Holmgren's successor before the season began.

Mora's tenure as head coach in Seattle lasted just one year, as the Seahawks went 5–11 on the heels of a 4–12 campaign in 2008, but while those were tumultuous times for the franchise, they would set up a reset at the top of the organization that would change the trajectory of the franchise in a big way, with Paul Allen hiring Carroll as head coach and John Schneider as general manager following the 2009 season, setting the table for the best decade in team history.

02 Born in Tacoma and a collegian at Central Washington, quarterback Jon Kitna played the first four seasons of his 14-year NFL career in his home state.

03 The Kingdome was imploded on March 26, 2000.

04

04 Defensive back Jordan Babineaux dives to stop Cowboys QB/holder Tony Romo after Romo muffed the snap on a game-winning field goal attempt with 1:14 left on the clock in Seattle's 21–20 victory in the 2006 Wild Card game.

05

06

07

05 All-Pro linebacker Chad Brown started all 107 games he played for the Seahawks.

06 Fullback Mack Strong played 201 games over 14 NFL seasons, all with the Seahawks.

07 Marcus Trufant gets to the ball before 49ers receiver Michael Crabtree.

#71

WALTER JONES

OFFENSIVE TACKLE

DATE INDUCTED
November 2, 2014

YEARS IN SEATTLE
1997–2009

COLLEGE
Florida State University

Walter Jones was the 11th member inducted into the Ring of Honor and the 10th player chosen. Since coming to Seattle as a first-round pick in 1997, Jones started all 180 games played while becoming the most dominant left tackle of his time. In 13 seasons, he was called for holding nine times and, in 5,703 pass attempts, surrendered just 23 sacks, according to coaches' statistics. He was selected to nine Pro Bowls (1999, 2001–08), passing Cortez Kennedy for most in team history, and was also a six-time AP All-Pro (1st Team in 2001, 2004, 2005, and 2007 and 2nd Team in 2006 and 2008). Seattle selected Jones with the sixth overall pick in the 1997 NFL Draft, which was acquired in a draft-day trade with the Tampa Bay Buccaneers in exchange for Seattle's first-round pick (#12, RB Warrick Dunn) and third-round pick (#66, CB Ronde Barber). Jones ranks fourth in Seattle history in games played (180) and second in games started (180). He became the first Seahawks player to reach double digits in postseason appearances and was inducted into the Pro Football Hall of Fame on August 2, 2014.

Riddell
71
SEATTLE
2 5
SEAHAWKS
71

08 Versatile and dependable Chris Gray played center and guard and missed only two games over a decade.

09 Chuck Darby reacts to making a play against the Rams.

10 Receiver Darrell Jackson hauls in a catch over Joselio Hanson of the 49ers.

08

09

10

11 Linebacker Lofa Tatupu pounds Buccaneers running back Carnell Williams to the ground.

11 →

Riddell
51
WILLIA

#8

MATT HASSELBECK

QUARTERBACK

DATE INDUCTED
October 25, 2021

YEARS IN SEATTLE
2001–2010

COLLEGE
Boston College

Matt Hasselbeck was the 13th member inducted into the Ring of Honor, and the 11th player chosen. Hasselbeck, who Mike Holmgren traded for as his hand-picked quarterback on March 2, 2001, started 131 of 138 regular-season games played and started all 11 postseason games played for Seattle from 2001 to 2010. He was a three-time Pro Bowler (2003, 2005, 2007), nine-time team captain (2001, 2003–10), the 2003 Seahawks Man of the Year, and the 2009 Largent Award recipient and led Seattle to its first Super Bowl appearance in 2005, with a franchise-best 13–3 record. He finished his time in Seattle as the franchise's all-time leader in attempts (4,250), completions (2,559), yards (29,434) and career wins (74), and second in touchdowns (174), numbers since surpassed by Russell Wilson. Hasselbeck finished his playing career with Tennessee (2011–12) and Indianapolis (2013–15), where he started 29 of 39 games played to end his career.

CHAMPIONS
SEAHAWKS
8

12 Quarterback Matt Hasselbeck holds up the NFC Championship trophy following the victory over the Carolina Panthers that sent the Seahawks to their first Super Bowl.

13

14

15

13 Joe Jurevicius contributed during his one season in Seattle, averaging 12.6 yards per reception and scoring 10 touchdowns.

14 In Super Bowl XL, Rocky Bernard clears the way as Kelly Herndon sprints 76 yards the other way after making an interception.

15 Shaun Alexander led all rushers with 95 yards in Super Bowl XL.

RING OF HONOR

#37

SHAUN ALEXANDER

RUNNING BACK

DATE INDUCTED
October 16, 2022

YEARS IN SEATTLE
2000–2007

COLLEGE
University of Alabama

Running back Shaun Alexander was inducted into the Seahawks Ring of Honor on October 16, 2022. He becomes the third member of Seattle's 2005 Super Bowl XL team to enter the Ring of Honor, joining Matt Hasselbeck and Mike Holmgren, who were inducted in 2021. Alexander, who scored an NFL-record five touchdowns in a half vs. Minnesota in 2002, ranks first in at least 20 career, season, or single-game franchise records, including rushing attempts (2,176), rushing yards (9,429), rushing touchdowns (100), total touchdowns (112), single-game rushing attempts (40), single-game rushing yards (266), single-game rushing touchdowns (4), and longest rush (88+). The 2005 AP NFL Most Valuable Player had a career year setting franchise records in attempts (370), yards (1,880), rushing touchdowns (27), and total touchdowns (28), leading Seattle to Super Bowl XL in Detroit. He was also Seattle's nominee for the Walter Payton NFL Man of the Year. Drafted 19th overall by Mike Holmgren in the 2000 NFL Draft, Alexander became a two-time AP All-Pro (second team in 2004; first team in 2005) and a three-time Pro Bowler (2003–05) and was voted to the NFL All-Decade Team of the 2000s. He started 96 of 119 regular-season games played and all nine postseason games played for Seattle from 2000 to 2007. Alexander finished his playing career in Washington (2008).

37

16 Leroy Hill racked up more than 500 tackles playing linebacker for Seattle.

17 Receiver Nate Burleson fights for yards after a catch against the Cardinals.

18 Defensive lineman Brandon Mebane appeared in 131 games over nine seasons with the Seahawks.

16

17

18

19 Cornerback Marcus Trufant keeps his eyes on the prize.

SEAHAWKS
GU
63

MIKE HOLMGREN

HEAD COACH

DATE INDUCTED
October 31, 2021

YEARS IN SEATTLE
1999–2008

LEGACY
2007 Horrigan Award recipient
2008 Largent Award recipient

Mike Holmgren was the 14th member inducted into the Ring of Honor, and the second head coach chosen. He was announced as executive vice president of football operations/general manager & head coach on January 8, 1999. He built Seattle into a perennial winner and Super Bowl contender to begin the decade. He acquired Matt Hasselbeck, drafted Hall of Fame guard Steve Hutchinson to team with Hall of Fame tackle Walter Jones, and drafted league MVP running back Shaun Alexander and starting wide receivers Darrell Jackson and Koren Robinson. His defenses featured John Randle, Chad Brown, Marcus Trufant, Ken Hamlin, and Lofa Tatupu. The Seahawks won five division titles (1999, 2004–07) and had a winning record in seven of his 10 seasons, with six playoff appearances and three 10-win seasons. In the previous 23 seasons before Holmgren's arrival, Seattle had a winning record eight times and won one division title, with four playoff appearances and two 10-win seasons. He was the winningest Seattle head coach, with a 90–80 combined record (regular & postseason) at the time of his departure. His teams recorded five consecutive winning seasons (2003–07) for the first time in franchise history and set the club's single-season record with 11 consecutive victories in 2005. Holmgren is one of five head coaches to take two different teams to a Super Bowl and win at least one title, and became the first coach in NFL history to record 75 or more wins with two franchises (Green Bay). Voted on by the Professional Football Writers of America, Holmgren was named the 2007 Horrigan Award Winner, given to the person (not a player or team media relations member) who helped the media best do its job during the season, and was the 2008 recipient of the Largent Award.

MOTOROLA

Riddell
76
SEAHAWKS
76

20

20 Hall of Fame offensive lineman Steve Hutchinson began his career in Seattle and played five seasons with the Seahawks.

21

22

23

21 Tim Ruskell was general manager of the Seahawks from 2005 to 2009 and helped lead the Seahawks to their first Super Bowl appearance.

22 Center Robbie Tobeck was named to the Pro Bowl the season that the Seahawks went to Super Bowl XL.

23 Jim Mora, head coach in 2009, and team CEO Tod Leiweke appear at a press conference.

12s

I've been a proud member of the 12s since the beginning, before the Seahawks even acknowledged the NFL's loudest, most enthusiastic fan base by becoming the only franchise to retire a jersey number for the fans. Since 1984, no Seahawk has worn number 12. It belongs to us, the group known as the 12s, just as we belong to the team and to this great city.

My name is Mike Stevens—that's me, pictured with my wife, Susie, at Super Bowl XLVIII—and in addition to being a member of the 12s, I am also one of the 50s—a select group of Seahawks season ticket holders since the team took flight in Seattle a half century ago.

When the Seahawks opened ticket sales to the old Kingdome in 1976, I was a 26-year-old small business owner who worked with engineers, architects, and developers. I bought my seats on the third day they were available, the day tickets sold out for the season. For the first few years, I sat in the upper level, behind the goalposts, and helped build something more fulfilling than any of the structures I worked on: a great tradition.

I have attended all but a handful of home games—at the Kingdome; Husky Stadium for two years; and Lumen Field since 2002—and every game, we'd watch opposing quarterbacks try to fend off the reverberating echoes from the 12s. Each snap was a false start or a mistimed route waiting to happen. The week before they'd play games in Seattle, visiting clubs used to practice with loud rock music in the background to prepare for the noise on gameday. During the NFC Wild Card game in 2011, we cheered so loudly, we caused an actual earthquake. After Marshawn Lynch broke eight tackles on a 67-yard touchdown run, the resulting eruption triggered a nearby seismograph. The moment became known as Beast Quake.

We had earned our celebrations because we endured the early frustrations that every young team experiences. Against the Rams in 1979, we recorded one first down, never crossed midfield, and posted a total offense of minus seven yards. That's still a record. The fans were a knowledgeable group. Our whole section had our notebooks out, keeping track of the yards. But we stuck it out despite the losses because the team was always entertaining, and we trusted things would get better.

Over the next decade, I had the perfect overhead view to appreciate Steve Largent's incomparable routes and receptions. We could see plays develop whenever he ran towards us. He was never that fast, and he didn't have great moves, but he always found space. He always got open. We'd say, "here he comes again, right at us." Everybody knew what was going to happen, but nobody on the opposing team knew how to stop him.

In January 2006, we finally won our first NFC title, crushing Carolina, 34–14. People got to the stadium at about nine o'clock that morning just to soak it all in, and the atmosphere outside the stadium was electric. I had goosebumps as soon as I got to the parking lot.

It took us eight more years before we got back to the Super Bowl. Midway through the season, my wife, Susie, and I made hotel and plane reservations to go to New York, hoping it would be our year. It was. We 12s worked our magic on the first play from scrimmage against the high-flying Broncos, when Denver's center couldn't hear the snap count amidst all the noise. As he looked over at our sections, the snap sailed over his head, and the play went for a safety. The rout was on from there.

We've moved our seats over the years, and we now sit above the 35-yard line. We'll see how many games we can make during the next 50 years, but we'll be here for as many as we can for as long as we can. We wouldn't want to miss a moment.

METLIFE STADIUM
SUPER BOWL
XLVIII
MetLife
pepsi
12

CAN YOU
HEAR
US NOW

LOUDER!

12

12
12
LOUD

1 2

CHAPTER FIVE

2010–2023

SEAHAWKS
SEAHAWKS
SEAHAWKS
SEAHAWKS
NFL
NFL
NFL
MOTOROLA
SEAHAWKS
31

For years, there had been speculation that Pete Carroll, in the midst of a wildly successful run at the University of Southern California, might return to the NFL, where he had previously been the head coach of the New York Jets and the New England Patriots before his dominant run in the college ranks.

And for years, that jump back into the NFL waters never happened, but just when it looked like Carroll might stay in college for good, Paul Allen and the Seahawks came calling after the 2009 season. Carroll, who wanted to return to the NFL only if he was going to be allowed to run a program the way he had done so successfully in college, was convinced by Allen and then–Seahawks CEO Tod Leiweke that the situation in Seattle was right for him, and in early January 2010, the Seahawks named Carroll their new head coach.

"I hope we can do things better than it's ever been done before around here," Carroll said in his introductory press conference after being named head coach. "Those are extraordinarily high expectations, and I love living in that world."

As Carroll noted, those were high expectations considering the run of success the Seahawks had enjoyed under Mike Holmgren in the previous decade, but they were expectations he and the franchise would ultimately live up to, as the Seahawks reached the postseason 10 times in 14 years, winning five NFC West titles, two NFC championships, and one Super Bowl, a dominant 43–8 win over the Broncos in Super Bowl XLVIII.

But before that success could come, Carroll and newly hired general manager John Schneider had a lot of work to do. They kicked off the turnround of the franchise with a 2010 draft class that helped lay the foundation for the team's future winning seasons. That spring, the Seahawks selected left tackle Russell Okung and safety Earl Thomas in the first round of the draft, receiver Golden Tate in the second round, cornerback Walter Thurmond in the fourth, and safety Kam Chancellor in the fifth—all players who would later make big contributions on a Super Bowl–winning team.

And the roster building was just beginning with that draft, as the Seahawks made a league-high 284

01 In a blockbuster hire, Pete Carroll joined the Seahawks in 2010 as head coach and executive vice president of football operations.

01

SEATTLE
SEAHAWKS
MOTOROLA
58
Reebok

transactions that year, including a franchise-altering trade in the middle of the season to acquire running back Marshawn Lynch.

The Seahawks finished the year with a 7–9 record, which in a down year for the NFC West was good enough to win a division title. Few gave the team, hosting the defending-champion New Orleans Saints, any chance in its first playoff game under Carroll, but led by a standout performance from Matt Hasselbeck in what would be the quarterback's final home game in Seattle, and punctuated by Lynch's famous 67-yard Beast Quake run, one of the great runs in NFL history, the Seahawks pulled off the upset. The Seahawks lost in Chicago in the divisional round, but already, the foundation was being laid for bigger things to come.

The Seahawks had another big draft class in 2011, adding cornerbacks Richard Sherman and Byron Maxwell, as well as linebackers K. J. Wright and future Super Bowl MVP Malcolm Smith, and they signed receiver Doug Baldwin as an undrafted free agent and cornerback Brandon Browner out of the Canadian Football League, moves that would lead to the birth of the Legion of Boom, a name first used as the nickname for Seattle's secondary that later came to define the entire team, with players using the initials *LOB* to also mean "Love Our Brothers."

The 2011 team finished 7–9 and missed the playoffs but finished the season strong as Lynch and the running game found their footing and the young defense showed a ton of potential. Then the 2012 draft brought even more key players, most notably linebacker Bobby Wagner and quarterback Russell Wilson, as well as defensive end Bruce Irvin, cornerback Jeremy Lane, and guard J. R. Sweezy.

Most observers thought the Seahawks would go with Matt Flynn, a free agent signing, as their quarterback, but Wilson won a competition between him, Flynn, and incumbent starter Tarvaris Jackson, beginning his 10-year run as Seattle's starter, which would see Wilson establish himself as the most accomplished quarterback in team history.

Behind a dominant defense that allowed the fewest points in the league, and standout play from the likes of Wilson, Lynch, and a young receiving corps, the Seahawks went 11–5 to earn a playoff berth, then won at Washington for Seattle's first playoff road win since the 1983 season. The following week, at Atlanta, the Seahawks nearly pulled off another road win but fell victim to the Falcons' late comeback. Despite the heartbreak of the loss, the Seahawks left Atlanta feeling like they were on the cusp of greatness.

As good as the Seahawks were in 2012, one area Carroll and Schneider wanted to improve was the team's pass rush, and in free agency, they signed Cliff Avril and Michael Bennett, two of the best free agent signings in team history, a day apart.

Given their ascending youth and strong finish in 2012, the Seahawks opened the 2013 season considered a Super Bowl contender, and they lived up to the hype, going 13–3 behind one of the best defenses in NFL history, a group that led the NFL in total defense, passing defense, takeaways, and points allowed.

With the No. 1 seed and homefield advantage, the Seahawks dispatched the Saints in the divisional round, then won a classic NFC Championship Game over the San Francisco 49ers, a game decided by one of the most famous and significant plays in franchise history: Sherman's pass breakup on a Colin Kaepernick throw in the end zone to Michael Crabtree, which Malcom Smith intercepted for a game-clinching touchdown.

That play, which would come to be known simply as the Tip, sent the Seahawks to Super Bowl XLVIII for a much-hyped matchup between the league's No. 1 defense and a Peyton Manning–led Broncos attack that was the highest-scoring offense in NFL history.

With a strong turnout from the 12s, MetLife Stadium was so loud that Denver's first play was a botched snap while Manning was still trying to change the play, resulting in a safety that kicked off one of the most dominant defensive performances in Super Bowl history. With the defense dominating and with Wilson and his receivers dialed in, the Seahawks built a big first-half lead, added to it with Percy Harvin's kick-return touchdown to open the second half, and rolled to one of the most lopsided wins in Super Bowl history despite Seattle facing an all-time great quarterback and offense.

Despite all the challenges that come with being a Super Bowl champ, the Seahawks earned the No. 1 seed again in 2014 and returned to the Super Bowl thanks to a thrilling overtime win over the Green Bay Packers in the NFC Championship Game, a win that featured a comeback from a 16-point deficit.

02

02 A week after hiring Pete Carroll, the Seahawks named John Schneider the team's general manager; he added the title of executive vice president in 2013 and today is the GM and president of football operations.

SMITH
53
31

03 A fifth-round draft pick in 2010, Kam Chancellor was a founding member of the Legion of Boom.

That made the Seahawks one of just three teams this century, along with the Patriots and the Kansas City Chiefs, to play in consecutive Super Bowls, but they were not able to repeat, falling just short after the Patriots erased a two-score deficit in the fourth quarter and then hung on when a game-winning pass attempt was intercepted at the goal line.

The following season saw the Seahawks start 0–2, an added dose of adversity after the heartbreaking finish to the previous season, but they rallied from there, finishing with a 10–6 record to return to the playoffs. Seattle once again led the league in scoring defense, making them the only team in the Super Bowl era to do so in four consecutive seasons. That season also was the first for another all-time great Seahawk, receiver Tyler Lockett, who as a rookie earned first-team All-Pro and Pro Bowl honors as a returner, and who would later go on to become the team's second-leading receiver in yards, receptions, and touchdowns, trailing only Hall of Famer Steve Largent.

During the Super Bowl, Lynch made his famous retirement announcement by posting a picture of his cleats hanging from a telephone wire, though after sitting out the 2016 season, he did return to play two seasons for the Oakland Raiders before making a brief return to Seattle late in the 2019 season. But that initial retirement marked the end of an era for one of the most significant players—and most interesting characters—in team history. Lynch, who Carroll pushed so hard to acquire in 2010, helped set a tone for the franchise that, along with the fierce play of the defense, made the Seahawks one of the most physical and feared teams in the league.

"He means everything to this offense," Baldwin said about Lynch prior to Super Bowl XLIX. "I don't know where we would be without Marshawn Lynch. He is the engine. He is the heart and soul of this offense. Everything runs through him."

Despite Lynch's retirement, the Seahawks were able to earn a fifth-straight playoff berth in 2016, winning the NFC West with a 10–5–1 record in a season that ended with a divisional-round loss in Atlanta.

The 2017 season marked the end of an era for the Seahawks, who went 9–7 but missed the playoffs for the first time since 2011. That season saw Sherman and Chancellor both suffer season-ending injuries in a Week 10 game in Arizona—injuries that, as it turned out, marked the end of their Seahawks careers: Sherman would be released the following offseason for salary-cap reasons, while Chancellor was forced to retire due to a neck injury.

The following year, another Legion of Boom original, Earl Thomas, broke his leg, also in Arizona, in what would be his final game as a Seahawk before he signed with Baltimore the following offseason. The 2018 team was able to return to the postseason with a 10–6 record but lost in the Wild Card round.

The 2018 season also came with some heartbreak for the franchise when Paul Allen, the Seahawks' owner and chairman, died at the age of 65 on October 15. Allen, the man who saved the Seahawks from relocation,

03

04

04 Richard Sherman soared from a fifth-round pick in 2011 to an All-Pro defensive back and one of the cornerstones of the Seahawks' fearsome defense.

05 A nine-time All-Pro and nine-time Pro Bowler, linebacker Bobby Wagner played 11 years as a Seahawk.

then helped build the team into one of the NFL's model franchises, was inducted into the Ring of Honor in 2019. Following Allen's death, his sister, Jody Allen, took over as Seahawks chair, allowing the organization to continue with steady leadership at the top that it has enjoyed since Paul Allen bought the team in 1997.

The 2019 offseason saw the Seahawks add future Pro Bowl receiver DK Metcalf with a second-round pick and sign Wilson to a contract extension that made him the league's highest-paid player at the time. With those two helping lead the way, the Seahawks went 11–5, falling inches short of a division title in a Week 17 loss to the 49ers, then won a playoff game at Philadelphia before losing in the divisional round at Green Bay.

In a 2020 season marked by empty stadiums, masks, and COVID-19 protocols, the Seahawks handled their business on the field, going 12–4 to win another NFC West crown, and they went the entire season without a player missing a game due to COVID-19.

After a 7–9 season in 2021, which included the first missed games of Wilson's career, the Seahawks made a pair of huge decisions in March 2022, releasing perennial All-Pro linebacker Bobby Wagner for salary-cap reasons and trading Wilson to the Broncos for a package that included a pair of first-round picks, two second-round picks, and three players.

Most observers were writing the team off in 2022 because of those moves, but with Geno Smith taking over the starting job, the Seahawks made it back to the playoffs, earning a Wild Card berth after going 9–8. Smith, who had been a backup for seven seasons before winning the job in 2022, threw for a then-franchise record 4,282 yards and was named the AP NFL Comeback Player of the Year and selected to his first Pro Bowl.

The Seahawks went 9–8 again in 2023, missing the playoffs this time, leading to a big offseason decision, as Carroll exited as head coach after 14 seasons, during which he compiled a 137–89–1 record, 10 playoff appearances, and the franchise's only Super Bowl title. Carroll, along with Schneider, also helped build a winning culture that has continued after his exit.

"What I am most proud of is that we took a culture that we developed in those college days and came here to see if you cared for people deeply and you loved them for who they were and tried to find the extraordinary uniqueness that made them, them, and celebrate that, and not try to make them something that they're not, and not to try to expect them to be something other than that, but try to see if we can capture that extraordinary uniqueness that they had, and celebrate that with them—let's see what happens," Carroll said. "Well, at USC, we killed it. And we came up here, and overall, we've been successful for a long time. I didn't think in any way this would happen like this. I didn't have that vision. But I'm grateful for it because what we have here is, we have an extraordinary culture. I'm really proud of that."

McQUISTAN
67
54
3

06 Russell Wilson proved to be the perfect quarterback for the Seahawks system. Elusive and accurate, Wilson was also durable, starting 158 games he played during a decade in Seattle.

07 All-Pro center Max Unger protects the pocket.

07

08 Chris Clemons fights off a block to get 49ers quarterback Alex Smith.

09 Cliff Avril celebrates after making a stop against the Saints.

08

09

10 Defensive end Michael Bennett recorded 39 sacks in the 75 games he played with Seattle.

10 →

72

17
24
78

11/12 **BEAST QUAKE**

In the 2010 NFC Wild Card game against New Orleans, Marshawn Lynch rambled for a 67-yard fourth-quarter touchdown, shedding eight Saints defenders and electrifying the 12s—so much so that the roaring and jumping of the fans inside the stadium registered a small tremor on a nearby seismic monitoring station.

12

13 Linebacker K.J. Wright tries to strip the ball from Patriots tight end Rob Gronkowski.

14 Seahawks receiver Golden Tate scores the game-winning touchdown on the infamous "Fail Mary" play.

13

14

15 **THE TIP**
Richard Sherman's perfectly timed deflection late in the 2013 NFC Championship Game saved a potential go-ahead touchdown by the 49ers, and Malcolm Smith's interception of the tipped ball sealed the victory and sent the Seahawks to Super Bowl XLVIII.

15

SHERMAN
25

SUPER BOWL
CHAMPIONS
MPIONS

16

16 Owner Paul G. Allen hoists the ultimate prize.

17

18

19

17 Malcolm Smith blasts past the Broncos' Louis Vasquez for a 69-yard pick-six in the second quarter of Super Bowl XLVIII. Smith was named the game's MVP.

18 Pete Carroll gets a celebratory dousing after guiding the Seahawks to a 43–8 drubbing of Denver for Seattle's first Super Bowl championship.

19 Nearly three-quarters of a million 12s packed downtown Seattle for the victory parade, the largest gathering in the city's history.

20 President Barack Obama poses with the Seahawks in the East Room of the White House.

PACKERS
42

21 Jermaine Kearse crosses the goal line with the game-winning touchdown in overtime to beat the Packers, 28–22, in the 2014 NFC Championship game.

22

23

24

22 Kam Chancellor and Russell Wilson recognize the 12s after earning a return trip to the Super Bowl.

23 Executing a fake field goal to perfection, holder (and punter) Jon Ryan throws a momentum-swinging 19-yard touchdown pass to eligible offensive tackle Garry Gilliam in the 2014 NFC Championship game.

24 Defensive back Earl Thomas and linebacker Bruce Irvin celebrate a stop during Super Bowl XLIX.

PAUL G. ALLEN

CHAIRMAN

DATE INDUCTED
October 3, 2019

YEARS IN SEATTLE
1997–2018

LEGACY
Founder and Chairman, Vulcan Inc.
Chairman, Vulcan Sports & Entertainment

Paul G. Allen was inducted to the Seahawks Ring of Honor on October 3, 2019. Allen, who passed away in October 2018 due to complications of non-Hodgkin's lymphoma, was the 12th member of the Ring of Honor. Under Allen's guidance, the Seahawks achieved new levels of success over two decades, first under head coach Mike Holmgren, who was one of Allen's most important early hires, and then under Pete Carroll and John Schneider, who Allen brought together in 2010. Prior to Allen purchasing the team, the Seahawks had eight winning seasons, won 10 or more games twice, earned four playoff berths, won their division once, and advanced to one AFC championship game. During Allen's ownership from 1997 to 2018, the Seahawks reached the postseason 13 times, won nine division titles, enjoyed nine seasons with 10 or more wins, and played in three Super Bowls, winning Super Bowl XLVIII to bring the Lombardi Trophy to Seattle for the first time. In addition to owning the Seahawks and the Portland Trail Blazers, Allen was a technology pioneer who co-founded Microsoft, then later launched Vulcan Inc., Stratolaunch Systems, the Allen Institute, and the Allen Institute for Artificial Intelligence. He was a philanthropist and conservationist who used his considerable wealth and influence to make a difference in so many ways around the world, giving more than $2.5 billion to causes near and dear to his heart; he enriched Seattle's art and music scene while also playing a mean guitar himself; he made amazing discoveries at the bottoms of oceans; he rebuilt Seattle's South Lake Union neighborhood; and he did so much more to make the Seattle area and the world a better and more interesting place.

25

25 Doug Baldwin played eight seasons in the NFL, all with Seattle, and led the NFL with 14 receiving touchdowns in 2015.

26 Paul Richardson hauls in an acrobatic touchdown versus Detroit in the 2016 NFC Wild Card game.

26

27 Offensive tackle Duane Brown played five of his 16 NFL seasons with the Seahawks, earning a Pro Bowl nod in 2021.

28 Running back Chris Carson gets airborne during a 116-yard rushing performance against the Rams in 2018.

29 Michael Dickson holds the franchise record for the highest career regular-season punt average, 48.2 yards, which ranks third all-time in the NFL.

28

27

29

30 Tyler Lockett gets both feet in for a toe-tap touchdown versus the Rams in 2019.

30 →

STARBUCKS
Sunday
HOME OF THE 12s

SEAHAWKS
SEAHAWKS

31 Quandre Diggs (6) and Coby Bryant (8) celebrate a Seahawks' defensive stop.

32 Kenneth Walker III beats 49ers linebacker Dre Greenlaw to the end zone in the 2022 NFC Wild Card game

32

33 Leonard Williams joined Seattle in a 2023 trade-deadline deal and made the Pro Bowl in 2024, earning the defensive lineman a three-year contract extension.

34 Linebacker Uchenna Nwosu wraps up Bears quarterback Caleb Williams.

35 Jarran Reed played his first five NFL seasons with Seattle and then, after two seasons with other teams, rejoined the Seahawks in 2023.

33

34

35

36 Devon Witherspoon was named NFC Defensive Player of the Week after having a highlight-reel game against the Giants in 2023, tallying seven tackles, three QB hits, two sacks, and a 97-yard pick-six.

36

21
54
0
ny

LEGION OF BOOM

EARL THOMAS
2010–2018

RICHARD SHERMAN
2011–2017

KAM CHANCELLOR
2010–2018

WALTER THURMOND
2010–2013

BRANDON BROWNER
2011–2013

BYRON MAXWELL
2011–2014, 2017

JEREMY LANE
2012–2017

DESHAWN SHEAD
2012–2017

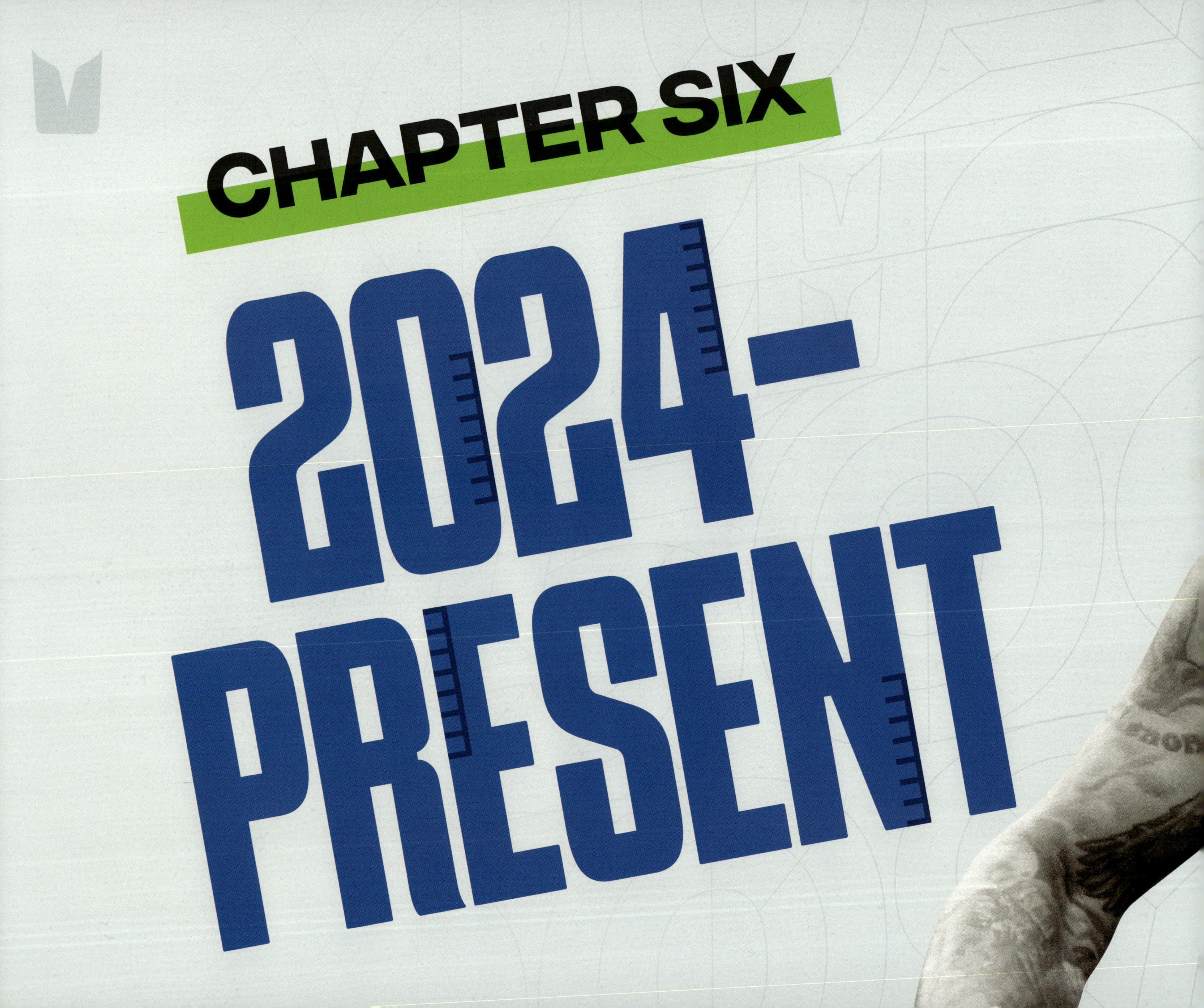

CHAPTER SIX

2024-PRESENT

SEAHAWKS
SEAHA
NFL
99

While the Seahawks missed the postseason in their final season under Pete Carroll, there were plenty of indicators, including the team's 9–8 record, that whoever succeeded Carroll in Seattle wouldn't be taking on a major rebuild. First, there was the winning culture Carroll and general manager John Schneider had built in their time together. Even before that, there was what the organization had done under Mike Holmgren. All this can be tied back to the leadership of former owner Paul Allen and, later, his sister, Jody Allen, who took over as chair of the Seahawks in 2018 following Paul Allen's death, eventually making the important decision to hire Mike Macdonald as Carroll's successor—a move that looks to have the Seahawks set up for continued success in the future.

There was also plenty of talent to work with on the roster, ranging from veteran standouts to recent draft picks from the 2022 and 2023 drafts that have helped the Seahawks build a new, young nucleus. By the end of the 2024 season, three players drafted in the previous two years—cornerbacks Riq Woolen and Devon Witherspoon and receiver Jaxon Smith-Njigba—had been selected as Pro Bowlers, and eight other players were either starters or playing significant roles on offense or defense: left tackle Charles Cross, outside linebacker Boye Mafe, running back Kenneth Walker III, right tackle Abraham Lucas, safety Coby Bryant, outside linebacker Derick Hall, running back Zach Charbonnet, and center Olu Oluwatimi.

With that young group in place, along with veterans like Geno Smith, DK Metcalf, Tyler Lockett, and Noah Fant on offense and Uchenna Nwosu, Leonard Williams, Jarran Reed, and Julian Love on defense, the organization was in a pretty good place for whoever was going to become the ninth head coach in franchise history.

Enter former Ravens defensive coordinator Mike Macdonald. At just 36 years old at the time of his hiring, Macdonald became the youngest head coach in the NFL, but despite his youth, he had impressive credentials, including two seasons as Baltimore's defensive coordinator, during which he had overseen one of the best and most innovative defenses in the league.

"This is the future right here," Schneider said when Macdonald was hired. "This is where it's going. I think you're going to learn in getting to know Mike that he's a special dude. This has happened quickly for him, but when you sit down with him and you get to meet him,

01 A first-round draft pick in 2023, receiver Jaxon Smith-Njigba had a breakout sophomore season, posting 1,130 receiving yards and tying a franchise record with 100 receptions.

01

SMITH-NJIG
7
52

you understand the why—the whys of, ‘Wow, he knows that guy, he knows that guy, and he knows this guy.’ I’ve been in the league for 30 years, and we know a ton of the same people. So that really stood out.

“He’s a disruptor—he’s changed it,” Schneider added. “You look at the product, look at their defense.”

Macdonald’s first season in Seattle included plenty of successes, including a 10–7 regular season record that made him the winningest first-year coach in franchise history. The Seahawks also went 7–1 on the road, matching a team record, finished strong, going 6–2 over the final eight games, made big strides on defense in the second half of the season, and sent three players—Witherspoon, Williams, and Smith-Njigba—to the Pro Bowl. But Macdonald and company weren’t satisfied with a season that saw them miss the postseason by the narrowest of margins, losing the tiebreaker for the NFC West title by the fifth tiebreaker—strength of victory—to the Rams. That being said, the future looks bright heading into the Seahawks’ 50th season and beyond.

“We’re just really optimistic, fired up for what’s ahead of us with the direction our team is going,” Macdonald said. “Obviously, we wanted to be fighting it out in the playoffs, and we felt like we had a good enough team to do some damage, but we didn’t earn the right to do that. So we’re moving on, but, man, we’re excited about what’s to come, working through what the offseason is going to look like, making some tweaks—how do we evolve? All that stuff’s ahead of us: how we build our roster—all those types of decisions, finding a new offensive coordinator, all those things. It’s an exciting time. I’m excited about the foundation that we’ve been able to lay and ready to get back to work.”

02

03

02 Seahawks chair Jody Allen, coach Mike Macdonald, and general manager John Schneider applaud a pick in the 2025 NFL Draft.

03 With the 16th pick in the 2024 NFL Draft, the Seahawks selected Byron Murphy II, a defensive lineman from the University of Texas.

04 The Seahawks swung a midseason trade with the Titans for Ernest Jones IV and then re-signed the linebacker to a three-year deal.

05 Quarterback Geno Smith took over as the starter in 2022, was named AP Comeback Player of the Year, and made his first Pro Bowl.

06 Six-foot-six-inch, 322-pound Everett native Abe Lucas is an imposing force on the offensive line.

04

05

06

07 The Seahawks defense celebrates an interception by defensive tackle Johnathan Hankins (97) against the 49ers.

07

Levi's
BUD LIGHT
BUDLIGHT
Foxconn Industrial Internet

AVILA
SEAHAWKS
20
SEAHAWKS
8

08 Defensive back Julian Love emerges excitedly with the ball after picking off the Rams.

09

10

11

09 The ninth overall pick in the 2022 NFL Draft, offensive tackle Charles Cross has started every game he has played in his three seasons in Seattle.

10 Edge rusher Boye Mafe pummels Falcons quarterback Kirk Cousins, causing a fumble returned for a touchdown by Seahawks teammate Derick Hall.

11 Receiver DK Metcalf scored 48 touchdowns in 93 games started over his six years with the Seahawks.

TOP 50 PLAYERS

As the Seahawks celebrate their 50th season in 2025, the team revealed its Top 50 Players in Seahawks history in June, voted upon by fans and a special panel of judges.

The list of eligible players included 163 players who have all played for the Seahawks at some point in their career and have met at least one of the criteria listed below:

- Started at least 45 games
- Voted to an AP All-Pro or NFL Pro Bowl team
- Won Seahawks Man of the Year or the Steve Largent Award
- Currently leads a career major statistical category, such as Most Receiving Yards in a Career
- Part of an iconic moment in Seahawks history

SHAUN ALEXANDER
CLIFF AVRIL
DOUG BALDWIN
EDWIN BAILEY
MICHAEL BENNETT
BRIAN BLADES
CHAD BROWN
DAVE BROWN
JEFF BRYANT
KEITH BUTLER
KAM CHANCELLOR
MICHAEL DICKSON
KENNY EASLEY
BOBBY ENGRAM
CHRIS GRAY
JACOB GREEN
JOHN HARRIS
MATT HASSELBECK
STEVE HUTCHINSON
DARRELL JACKSON
WALTER JONES
CORTEZ KENNEDY
DAVE KRIEG
STEVE LARGENT
TYLER LOCKETT
MARSHAWN LYNCH
BRANDON MEBANE
DK METCALF
BRYAN MILLARD
JOE NASH
RUFUS PORTER
EUGENE ROBINSON
JON RYAN
RICHARD SHERMAN
MICHAEL SINCLAIR
MACK STRONG
LOFA TATUPU
EARL THOMAS III
ROBBIE TOBECK
MARCUS TRUFANT
MAX UNGER
BOBBY WAGNER
CURT WARNER
CHRIS WARREN
JOHN L. WILLIAMS
RUSSELL WILSON
DEVON WITHERSPOON
K.J. WRIGHT
FREDD YOUNG
JIM ZORN

SEAHAWKS

SKYBOX PRESS

Editor & Publisher
Scott Gummer

Design
SeeSullivan

Photo Editor
Rebecca Butala How

Copyeditor
Mark Nichol

Contributing Editors
Brian Cazeneuve
Ryan Hunt

Contributing Writer
John Boyle

Special thanks to Tyson Flandreau, Jeff Garza, Doug Orwiler, and John Weaver with the Seahawks; Kevin O'Sullivan with Associated Press; Carmin Romanelli, Michael Klein, Mark Awad, and Daniel Romo at Getty Images; and Chris Gruener.

PHOTOGRAPHY

ASSOCIATED PRESS: Al Messerschmidt, Allen Kee, Damian Strohmeyer, David Stluka, Ed Wolfstein/IconSportswire, Elaine Thompson, Eric Lars Bakke, G.Newman Lowrance, Greg Trott, Kevin Terrell, Paul Abell, Paul Jasienski, Paul Spinelli, Peter Read Miller, Ric Tapia, Ron Riesterer, Scott Boehm, Todd Rosenberg, Vernon Biever, AP Photo

GETTY IMAGES: Getty Images Sport Andy Lyons, Arthur Anderson, Chip Somodevilla, Damian Strohmeyer, Daniel Sheehan, Elsa, George Gojkovich, George Rose, Gin Ellis, Harry How, Jane Gershovich, Jed Jacobsohn, Jonathan Ferrey, Kirby Lee, Michael Zagaris, Miguel A. Elliot, Mitchell Layton, Otto Greule Jr., Rick Stewart, Rob Carr, Steph Chambers, Stephen Dunn, Thearon W. Henderson, Tim DeFrisco, Tom Hauck; **Hulton Archive** Brian Bahr; **Tribune News Service** Sacramento Bee; **Focus on Sport**; **Icon Sportswire**; **Sporting News**

Additional photography contributed by the Seattle Seahawks and Mike Stevens

www.skyboxpress.com
info@skyboxpress.com

ISBN: 979-8-9921084-1-5

Printed in the United States of America

10 9 8 7 6 5 4 3 2 1

Published by Skybox Press, LLC.